An Alzheimer's Caregiver Prayer "Stations of the Cross" & Divine Mercy Chaplet

Spiritual Meditation for an Alzheimer's caregiver

By:
Roy P. Poillon
4th Degree Knight of Columbus
Cleveland, Ohio

In your Journey to the cross consider

"He who would climb to a lofty height must go by steps, not leaps".
Pope St. Gregory the Great

In my spiritual journey as a caregiver, these words of Pope St. Gregory the Great hold wisdom in how I need to approach my presentation to the Lord in my suffering as a giver of care for my loved one with Alzheimer's.

The Stations of the Cross:

1. Jesus condemned to death

2. Jesus carries his cross

3. Our Lord falls the first time

4. Jesus meets his mother

 5. Simon the Cyrenean helps Jesus carry his cross

6. Veronica wipes the face of Jesus

7. The second fall of Jesus

8. Jesus consoles the women of Jerusalem

9. The third fall of Jesus

10. Jesus is stripped of his garments

11. Jesus is nailed to the cross

12. Jesus dies on the cross

13. Jesus is taken down from the cross

14. Jesus is laid in the tomb

We all belong to Him, One in the Body: "For as the body is one and has many members, but all the members of that one body, being many, are one body, so also is Christ". 1 Corinthians 12:12

Therefore, to live this journey I am but one part of Christ's plan in serving the needs of my loved one with Alzheimer's disease. My gifts will be freely used and I pray for the strength to live this journey in a way that is pleasing to Him. I commit myself to serve as one of the many members, of that one body, in the Lord Jesus Christ.

Preparing for an Act of Contrition

A prayer for my faith journey

Latria: "This is my veneration that is due to God alone for His supreme excellence and I will show my complete submission to you Lord. It is my essential adoration. In my latria I give myself to God, as the Trinity. Amen"

Scripture: "16. Therefore, we do not lose heart. Though outwardly we are wasting away, yet inwardly we are being renewed day by day. 17. For our light and momentary troubles are achieving for us an eternal glory that far outweighs them all. 18. So we fix our eyes not on what is seen, but on what is unseen, since what is seen is temporary, but what is unseen is eternal".. 2 Corinthians 4: 16-18

"For this I am joyous Lord that I am so loved by you, to have me travel a pathway that brings me closer to you".

Colossians 1:24 Paul asserts, "I am now rejoicing in my sufferings for your sake, and in my flesh I am completing what is lacking in Christ's afflictions for the sake of his body, that is, the church."

Paul reminds us that the world is not complete and not perfect and that through Christ's suffering we are redeemed. Because it is not complete we are called to be coworkers with Christ. And he tells us, what we do for him, by including him, whatever we ask for the good of His work will be given.

Reflections: *We offer our suffering to Jesus, He takes the suffering and transforms it into the love for someone else, like an intercessory prayer. This redemptive suffering is a way to dedicate my sacrifice that it may benefit the one I love or that someone.*

My Statement in Faith:
I do not abstain or resist this offer to heal and develop my soul. For resistance to the Will of Heaven in the crosses of life is a missed opportunity toward developing my spirit. We are all calculated to be connected to suffering. Where by doing good works, to receive the joys of eternal glory; and from our heart we unite with him, following His passion in the diminishment of Alzheimer's disease.

For our Loved One:
"Dementia may take away the brain and the body, but it cannot steal the soul." "No Act of Love is Every Wasted" Jane Thibault & Richard Morgan

Station 1: Christ is sentenced to death by Pilate

Our Reflection:

In each stage of this Alzheimer's disease I am faced with new challenges that I am not prepared to handle, but I know that you Lord have prepared a plan that I am to live and experience. In the same way, Christ faced his new challenges of dying on the Cross, I too am facing mine

The Mystery:

The First Station of the Cross; here is my soul's redeemer, receiving a sentence to be scourged and committed to death. He knows what this passion will require and yet willingly he accepts his father's command to complete his fate.

As I find myself assigned to be the partner of a dying loved one, I too prepare myself for this journey. It is from my spirit and flesh that I pray for His Divine Mercy and move forward into the next phase of my journey as a caregiver. "For I know the plans I have for you," declares the Lord, "plans to prosper you and not to harm you, plans to give you hope and a future." – Jeremiah 29:11

The Prayer:

"Lord, I place myself into your hands. Let your love take possession of my heart; let what I see in my loved one behold the Love and affections that are from you; let my ears be open to your words of care and compassion turning away from the face the heedless remarks of what others may say that is hurtful to me. Have Mercy on me Lord. Give to me your grace!"
Hail Mary

Station 2: Christ takes the Cross on his shoulder

Our Reflection:

The cross makes me aware that this is not a life journey that I sought out, but that God loves me so much, wants to develop me so greatly, and seeks to give me this journey. Without my cross on my shoulders, I would not appreciate what Mercy He gives me.

The Mystery:

The second Station of the Cross; is when the heavy burden of the Cross is placed on His scourged shoulders to carry forward. With a silent patience. Let me reflect on my sensitive pride as I experience their dementia related behavior.

Luke 10: 28-30 **28.** Come to me, all you that labor, and are burdened, and I will refresh you. **29** Take up my yoke upon you, and learn of me, because I am meek, and humble of heart: and you shall find rest to your souls. **30.** For my yoke is sweet and my burden light.

The Prayer:

Heavenly Father, here on earth you breathe heavy under the burden of the cross. For it is new to your shoulders to bare. I am also new to my task and I am in need for your forgiveness because I am weak, strengthen me Lord from the pain. That I may grow to be more than myself. Help me Lord to continue your plan for my life now with this cross of being a caregiver for the one that I love so dearly. *Hail Mary*

Station 3: Jesus falls the first time under the Cross

Our Reflection:

At times we feel that life beats on us while we are already struggling to stay on the path of doing what is good and right. Why does this journey need to be even more difficult than it already is?

The Mystery:

This third Station shows us how Jesus was overwhelmed by the weight of His Cross. This causes us to consider the patience of the Lamb, receiving the insults and blows by those that attacked him for His truth. "If anyone would come to me, he must deny himself and take up his cross daily and follow me". (Luke 9:23).

The Prayer:

"Lord, I pause here to feel the pain of rejection, physical exhaustion both yours and mine as a Caregiver. Will I persevere in my passion to serve in your love for the one I love, on their path of diminishment? I will refuse to submit to abandoning my commitment to compassion, kindness and acts of selfless loves. Let me not seek a different path than what you are guiding me through. Please Lord, because with your cross you continued, now so shall I. Jesus! stretch out your hand to my assistance, that I may never more fall into the doubting of your loving care for me and my loved one; that I may at all times harken to your voice. *Hail Mary*

Station 4: Jesus meets His afflicted Mother

Our Reflection:

A part of this journey includes me coming closer to Him through my suffering. In my struggles caring for my loved one with Alzheimer's, give me a time to ponder the likeness of how I can use His passion as my own. May I also see and experience the love that this gives me, so it can be shared for all. For I know that in my challenges I am given His Love for many of those that love me to experience.

The Mystery:

The fourth Station helps us to connect with the desolation that our Lords' Mother felt in her suffering. This rent her soul, when she beheld Her beloved son. I consider my journey and see the parallel of lives lived in this suffering. "Trust in the Lord with all your heart and lean not on your own understanding; in all ways acknowledge Him, and He will make your paths straight" (Proverbs 3:5-6).

The Prayer:

Mournful Mother! You are a fountain of love! Let me feel your mystery of love's power that gave you strength in your life journey. I long for such love and such peace as you had in your hours of caring while your son suffered in front of you. Such compassion, stirs in the depths of my heart for you Blessed Mother and what you experienced. *Hail Mary*

Station 5: Christ assisted by Simon to carry His Cross

Our Reflection:

How many times have we come to the aid of others? Jesus allows another to help Him carry His cross, the cross that is not His but for others. Help me Lord to allow others to come inside my journey to help me. Give me your Mercy Lord.

The Mystery:

The fifth Station represents Christ fainting strength, giving to another is my opportunity to demonstrate how I am compassionate. So others may see in my time of need, this is a shameless commitment. It is for me to do these acts, because I do them in your name for someone that cannot do for themselves and for others to me in my journey.

The Prayer:

O suffering Jesus! To what excess did you go to give us a living example of how our struggles are shared as an example for others to understand? Make me so I am willing to let them take hold. Give me the heart to receive help in my journey as a caregiver, in a way that pleases you.
Hail Mary

Station 6: Veronica presents a cloth to Christ

Our Reflection:

At times it takes another person to help us see ourselves in our situation. Here too the lord is refreshed and is reminded of what this situation looks like. I need to allow those that I trust, give me input on my journey.

The Mystery:

The sixth Station represents Veronica, compassionating His agony as Redeemer, beholding His sacred face as a result of his journey in the presents of a cloth with which Jesus wipes His face. Am I willing to allow others to wipe away my blood in this journey as I bare the cross of a caregiver? Can I return in this singular grace that which He gave me at this station? Philippians 2:3-4: "Let nothing be done through selfish ambition or conceit, but in lowliness of mind let each esteem others better than himself".

The Prayer:

O Jesus, grant me tears to weep my ingratitude away, to what this journey means to my soul. Lift up my head, wipe my eyes clear, and help me to see the joy that is here because it is now that I draw closer to you in this journey of Alzheimer's. *Hail Mary*

Station 7: Jesus falls the second time

Our Reflection:

How many times will I stumble and fall? How often will I make mistakes and still be required to get up and continue? How heavy is my cross that it interrupts my life. The paths behind me are gone, the way ahead is unknown, and towards this act of mercy I push forward as a caregiver for my loved one.

The Mystery:

The seventh Station represents the gate of Jerusalem, called the gate of Judgment. At the entrance our Savior, through anguish and weakness, falls to the ground. How will I be judged as a caregiver, how am I to judge myself? Can I be accomplished enough to make judgements on myself or is this left to Christ, my Redeemer?

The Prayer:

O Most Holy Redeemer! Forgive my utmost contempt to rationalize the judgement of others. Deprive me of fame and honor for what I do so that as a caregiver my acts are in pure love and devotion to you. *Hail Mary*

Station 8: The Women of Jerusalem Console Jesus

Our Reflection:

Allowing others to care about me means understanding their need to show me their love. Part of my journey as a caregiver is to be an example that in my suffering, my ability to share with others is an added burden, but for them to participate is a blessing. I desire to let others see my journey, see how Jesus Christ is here with me and share how this has helped me grow my soul and spirit.

The Mystery:

The Eighth Station represents the place where several devout women meeting Jesus, and beholding Him wounded and bathed in His blood, shed tears of compassion over Him. Yes, I will obey my suffering Lord, and pour out tears of compassion. Few things are more eloquent than the voice of those whose tears flow from their struggle in the care of their loved one with Alzheimer's disease. How long the journey, how many questions seem to go unanswered?

The Prayer:

O Jesus, only begotten Son of the Father! I humbly beseech Thee by my tears that you soften my unity with you Lord. That I may know that this caregiving I do for you and that I am not alone. *Hail Mary*

Station 9: Jesus falls under the Cross the third time

Our Reflection:

Now I see how truly heavy this cross is, as I reflect on all that it asks of me. I rest in exhaustion, I live my day in confusion as I practice the care which I create. This is a new care, required to meet the needs of my loved one, each and every day. Yet, I know that I must continue, as so did Jesus, in this His third fall.

The Mystery:

This Station represents the foot of Mount Calvary, where Jesus Christ, destitute of strength, falls a third time to the ground. The anguish of His wounds is renewed. I learn here that all of myself must be given to God if I am to truly receive all of His Mercy and Grace. Sometimes my exhaustion comes from me fighting to let go of myself, even though I know that letting go is to be done in order that my Lord and Savior can take charge.

The Prayer:

O Jesus! I return to you in infinite thanks for not permitting me to lay down and remain with my journey uncompleted. Help me each time that I fall to get up and continue to journey according to your plan for me and my loved one. *Hail Mary*

Station 10: Jesus is stripped of His Garments

Our Reflection:

When I put on my clothes, get into my car and live in my house I hide in my image of what is me. I do this so others may not see the real me. This journey with Alzheimer's is stripping away those areas that I used to hide from others. Do I dare uncover and remove what covers me? Or stand in humility knowing that I belong to Jesus Christ. It is His judgement alone that I stand in front of to receive His mercy so I may live in forgiveness. Being a giver of care in Alzheimer's requires humility.

The Mystery:

The Tenth Station represents the humility of death. If in death those things that I am "holding on to that which are not mine", then by doing this I release to God those things of mine which He has asked to carry for me. From this I become available to receive what is truly His. And in this I desire to stand in front of the Lord my God, without the pretenses of humanity. Free of what is not mine, I choose to stand in humility in front of you Lord.

The Prayer:

Suffering Jesus! I behold Thee stripped to expose your humility, grant me such strength that I may relinquish all that holds me back in receiving your Mercy and Grace. *Hail Mary*

Station 11: Christ is nailed to the Cross

Our Reflection:

These nails represent the final commitment to the act of love. Lord, In the same I take up my role. My nails are set into place as a commitment to you Lord, so that I may become your instrument.

The Mystery:

This Eleventh Station represents the place where Jesus Christ, in the presence of His Mother, is stretched on the Cross, and nailed to it. Consider His exhaustion, the anguish of His Mother, the unfairness of His suffering. He bore the cost and fulfills His plan which the father put before Him. I now seek my cross in life with ready resignation to the will of God.

The Prayer

O patient Jesus! Meek Lamb of God! Who promised, "When I shall be exalted from earth I will draw all things to myself". I now renounce and detest my past impatience. Let me crucify my flesh and the anger that I have surrounding my loved ones dementia related behavior. That I may be renewed and serve you, Lord, as I serve the needs of my loved one. _Hail Mary_

Station 12: Christ is exalted on the Cross, and dies

Our Reflection:

There comes my suffering as it is now of myself. Is this something that I am called to let go of for His sake. At this station I am now letting the "Me" in suffering die to Him who asked for it. Because He died for my sins, I can now release what is not mine. I am leaving my suffering, here, at the foot of the cross.

The Mystery:

This Twelfth Station represents the place where Jesus Christ was publicly exalted on the Cross. But this was not the final act. However, it needed to take place in this sequence for us to recognize that this is the final part of his suffering, it stops here as we know it. I desire to separate my agony, in order to release it to you Lord. In replacement for His charity and triumphs over His agony, I become His triumph over my agony. He continues this closure by inviting me into a direct relationship with His mother, Blessed Holy Mary Mother of God. Then he commended His soul to the father.

The Prayer:

Help me Lord to stop my suffering as I now know it to be mine, I freely give this to you for your greater glory. Lord I praise your name as we move together as one.   *Hail Mary*

Station 13: Christ is taken down from the Cross

Our Reflection:

As we dismantle my suffering in being who I am and having now given it over to God, I see a broken shell of misery and torment, which actually never was mine to hold onto.

The Mystery:

The Thirteenth Station represents the place where Christ's most sacred body was taken down from the Cross by Joseph and Nicodemus, and laid in the care of His weeping Mother.

Now what remains would appear to be just my love for Jesus and His love for me. But now so much more is released. He has established a new understanding of how my suffering is for others and from this it allows me a closer union with God.

The Prayer:

Lord, in whatever way I may survive this journey and survive it I will do. I give thanks and praise to you Lord for all you did on the cross in giving of yourself so that I may have you to give my suffering too. Praise and Glory to you oh Lord for you are kind and forgiving. Replace my suffering as a caregiver, now with your Divine Love and Mercy. *Hail Mary*

Station 14: Christ is laid in the Tomb

Our Reflection:

Now I am free to rise again and continue in the renewed spirit of Jesus Christ. I am forgiven at the foot of the cross, I leave my suffering there and receive His Mercy.

The Mystery:

The Fourteenth Station represents Christ's Sepulcher, and the love and devotion when His blessed body was laid with respect. Now my devotion to Him causes me to become joined in His love that I may be strong again to face what comes next in this journey with Alzheimer's. I do so knowing that I have the righteousness of Jesus Christ, the protection of the Holy Spirit and foundation of the Lord's commandments. And that I am justified in following this life pathway that he has planned for me.

The Prayer:

Charitable Jesus, for my salvation you performed this passion of love; this painful journey of the Cross. Let me press forward in my gaining what is pleasing to you in all that I do. Give me your wisdom, courage and love to share as a caregiver. Use me as you so desire, in my continued journey with my loved one. Have mercy on us all. One Our Father, *Hail Mary Sign of the Cross. Amen.*

The Anima Christi

Soul of Christ,   sanctify me
Body of Christ,   save me
Blood of Christ, inebriate me
Water from Christ's side,   wash me
Passion of Christ,   strengthen me
O good Jesus,   hear me
Within Thy wounds,   hide me
Suffer me not,   to be separated from Thee
From the malicious enemy, defend me
In the hour of my death,   call me
And bid me,   come unto Thee

That I may praise Thee with Thy saints
and with Thy angels

Forever and ever

Stations of the Cross Log

Date: _____ **Location**

_____

_____

_____

_____

_____

_____

_____

_____

_____

_____

_____

_____

_____

_____

_____

_____

_____

_____

_____

_____

Divine Mercy Chaplet

An Alzheimer's Journey in the
Divine Mercy

Jesus, I Trust in You

Jesus, I trust in You

Following the Divine Mercy message:

A - Ask for His Mercy. God wants you to approach Him in prayer constantly.

B - Be merciful. God wants you to receive His Mercy. And to share it with others.

C – Consistently trust in Jesus. God wants us to come to Him consistently, with confidence that we do trust in Him.

As a caregiver of a loved one with Alzheimer's we need to trust in Him, by asking for His mercy, consistently throughout our journey.

You can follow this on Youtube:
https://www.youtube.com/watch?v=Rbw4QuGksXA

Numbers are in accordance with Rosary steps

Sign of the Cross (holding the cross)
In the name of the Father, and of the Son, and of the Holy Spirit. Amen.

Opening Prayer (optional)
You expired Jesus, but a source of life gushes forth for souls, and the ocean of mercy opened up for the whole world. O Fount of Life, unfathomable Divine Mercy, envelop the whole world and empty yourself out upon us.

Our Father (first bead)
1. Our Father Our Father, who art in heaven, hallowed be Thy name; Thy kingdom come; Thy will be done on earth as it is in heaven. Give us this day our daily bread; and forgive us our trespasses as we forgive those who trespass against us; and lead us not into temptation, but deliver us from evil, Amen.

Hail Mary (second bead)
2. Hail Mary, full of grace. The Lord is with thee. Blessed art thou amongst women, and blessed is the fruit of thy womb, Jesus. Holy Mary, Mother of God, pray for us sinners, now and at the hour of our death, Amen.

The Apostle's Creed (third bead)
3. I believe in God, the Father Almighty, creator of heaven and earth. and in Jesus Christ, His only Son, our Lord, who was conceived by the Holy Spirit, and born of the Virgin Mary, suffered under Pontius Pilate, was crucified, died, and was buried; he descended into hell; on the third day he rose again from the dead; he ascended into heaven, and is seated at the right hand of God the Father almighty; from there he will come again to judge the living and the dead. I believe in the Holy Spirit, the holy Catholic Church, the communion of saints, the forgiveness of sins, the resurrection of the body, and the life everlasting. Amen.

The Eternal Father (fourth bead)

4. Eternal Father, I offer you the Body and Blood, Soul and Divinity of Your Dearly Beloved Son, Our Lord, Jesus Christ, in atonement for our sins and those of the whole world.

On the next Ten Small Beads of this First Decade

5. Pray: "For the sake of His sorrowful Passion, have mercy on us and on the whole world".

6. Pray: "For the sake of His sorrowful Passion, have mercy on us and on the whole world".

7. Pray: "For the sake of His sorrowful Passion, have mercy on us and on the whole world".

8. Pray: "For the sake of His sorrowful Passion, have mercy on us and on the whole world".

9. Pray: "For the sake of His sorrowful Passion, have mercy on us and on the whole world".

10. Pray: "For the sake of His sorrowful Passion, have mercy on us and on the whole world".

11. Pray: "For the sake of His sorrowful Passion, have mercy on us and on the whole world".

12. Pray: "For the sake of His sorrowful Passion, have mercy on us and on the whole world".

13. Pray: "For the sake of His sorrowful Passion, have mercy on us and on the whole world".

14. Pray: "For the sake of His sorrowful Passion, have mercy on us and on the whole world".

The Eternal Father (the our father bead)

15. Eternal Father, I offer you the Body and Blood, Soul and Divinity of Your Dearly Beloved Son, Our Lord, Jesus Christ, in atonement for our sins and those of the whole world.

On the next Ten Small Beads of This Second Decade

16. Pray: "For the sake of His sorrowful Passion, have mercy on us and on the whole world".

17. Pray: "For the sake of His sorrowful Passion, have mercy on us and on the whole world".

18. Pray: "For the sake of His sorrowful Passion, have mercy on us and on the whole world".

19. Pray: "For the sake of His sorrowful Passion, have mercy on us and on the whole world".

20. Pray: "For the sake of His sorrowful Passion, have mercy on us and on the whole world".

21. Pray: "For the sake of His sorrowful Passion, have mercy on us and on the whole world".

22. Pray: "For the sake of His sorrowful Passion, have mercy on us and on the whole world".

23. Pray: "For the sake of His sorrowful Passion, have mercy on us and on the whole world".

24. Pray: "For the sake of His sorrowful Passion, have mercy on us and on the whole world".

25. Pray: "For the sake of His sorrowful Passion, have mercy on us and on the whole world".

The Eternal Father

Eternal Father, I offer you the Body and Blood, Soul and Divinity of Your Dearly Beloved Son, Our Lord, Jesus Christ, in atonement for our sins and those of the whole world.

On the next Ten Small Beads of This Third Decade

26Pray: "For the sake of His sorrowful Passion, have mercy on us and on the whole world".

27. Pray: "For the sake of His sorrowful Passion, have mercy on us and on the whole world".

28. Pray: "For the sake of His sorrowful Passion, have mercy on us and on the whole world".

29. Pray: "For the sake of His sorrowful Passion, have mercy on us and on the whole world".

30. Pray: "For the sake of His sorrowful Passion, have mercy on us and on the whole world".

31. Pray: "For the sake of His sorrowful Passion, have mercy on us and on the whole world".

32. Pray: "For the sake of His sorrowful Passion, have mercy on us and on the whole world".

33. Pray: "For the sake of His sorrowful Passion, have mercy on us and on the whole world".

34. Pray: "For the sake of His sorrowful Passion, have mercy on us and on the whole world".

35. Pray: "For the sake of His sorrowful Passion, have mercy on us and on the whole world".

The Eternal Father

36. Eternal Father, I offer you the Body and Blood, Soul and Divinity of Your Dearly Beloved Son, Our Lord, Jesus Christ, in atonement for our sins and those of the whole world.

On the next Ten Small Beads of This Fourth Decade

37. Pray: "For the sake of His sorrowful Passion, have mercy on us and on the whole world".

38. Pray: "For the sake of His sorrowful Passion, have mercy on us and on the whole world".

39. Pray: "For the sake of His sorrowful Passion, have mercy on us and on the whole world".

40. Pray: "For the sake of His sorrowful Passion, have mercy on us and on the whole world".

41. Pray: "For the sake of His sorrowful Passion, have mercy on us and on the whole world".

42. Pray: "For the sake of His sorrowful Passion, have mercy on us and on the whole world".

43. Pray: "For the sake of His sorrowful Passion, have mercy on us and on the whole world".

44. Pray: "For the sake of His sorrowful Passion, have mercy on us and on the whole world".

45. Pray: "For the sake of His sorrowful Passion, have mercy on us and on the whole world".

46. Pray: "For the sake of His sorrowful Passion, have mercy on us and on the whole world".

The Eternal Father

47. Eternal Father, I offer you the Body and Blood, Soul and Divinity of Your Dearly Beloved Son, Our Lord, Jesus Christ, in atonement for our sins and those of the whole world.

On the next Ten Small Beads of This Fifth Decade

48. Pray: "For the sake of His sorrowful Passion, have mercy on us and on the whole world".

49. Pray: "For the sake of His sorrowful Passion, have mercy on us and on the whole world".

50. Pray: "For the sake of His sorrowful Passion, have mercy on us and on the whole world".

51. Pray: "For the sake of His sorrowful Passion, have mercy on us and on the whole world".

52. Pray: "For the sake of His sorrowful Passion, have mercy on us and on the whole world".

53. Pray: "For the sake of His sorrowful Passion, have mercy on us and on the whole world".

54. Pray: "For the sake of His sorrowful Passion, have mercy on us and on the whole world".

55. Pray: "For the sake of His sorrowful Passion, have mercy on us and on the whole world".

56. Pray: "For the sake of His sorrowful Passion, have mercy on us and on the whole world".

57. Pray: "For the sake of His sorrowful Passion, have mercy on us and on the whole world".

Concluding Prayer (repeat three times)

Holy God, Holy Mighty One, Holy Immortal One, have mercy on us and on the whole world.

Holy God, Holy Mighty One, Holy Immortal One, have mercy on us and on the whole world.

Holy God, Holy Mighty One, Holy Immortal One, have mercy on us and on the whole world.

Closing Prayer

Eternal God, in whom mercy is endless and the treasury of compassion — inexhaustible, look kindly upon me and increase your mercy in me, that in difficult moments we might not despair nor become despondent, but with great confidence submit ourselves to your holy will, which is Love and Mercy itself

Sign of the Cross

In the name of the Father, and of the Son, and of the Holy Spirit. Amen.

Divine Mercy Chaplet Log

Date: _____ **Location**

_____

_____

_____

_____

_____

_____

_____

_____

_____

_____

_____

_____

_____

_____

_____

_____

_____

_____

R~ House
Alzheimer's Family Learning Center

Order these Prayer Books:
Alzheimer's Caregiver Station of the Cross

Alzheimer's Caregiver Rosary

For your Family Members Order:
7 Dynamics in an Alzheimer's Family
The Alzheimer's Journey, It's Time to Get Organized
The Alzheimer's Journey, Connecting the Puzzle Pieces,
(learn each stage)

For your Church or Parish Order:
Alzheimer's Inside the Parish Gates Seminar; Pastor, Deacon, Lay
Ministry Leaders Training about Alzheimer's
&
"Alzheimer's Outreach Ministry" Model a turn key program

Website: http://www.spiritualpathwaysinalzheimers.com/order-now/

Call Us: (440) 385-7605 **Email:** wittsendconsulting@gmail.com

On Line Resources

Alzheimer's Association (both National and local chapters)

www.alzheimersassociation.org

This is your primary site for extensive information on Alzheimer's

(800) 272-3900

Learn like a professional, Get ready for what's ahead.

HealthCare Interactive On Line Dementia Care Training

www.hcinterative.com

(952) 928-7722

Taking their On-Line courses in dementia related behavior is the family caregiver's best way to prepare yourself for the challenges that will be a part of your journey.

www.Youtube.com

Search for: Teepa Snow

www.ingramcontent.com/pod-product-compliance
Lightning Source LLC
Chambersburg PA
CBHW041759040426
42447CB00001B/26